Two Cats and a Pen

Nida Anwer

BookLeaf
Publishing

India | USA | UK

Presentation by *BookLeaf Publishing*

Web: www.bookleafpub.com

E-mail: info@bookleafpub.com

ISBN : 9789357449168

First edition 2021

Is It Really That Bad?

Sad
I get hurt
although it's pain
in some way I gain
to grow into something more
maybe it isn't so bad at all
lonley
wanting a hug
and after all that waiting
it's like a painting
it's there and I can see it
but I can't feel it
not just yet
but time will tell
my heart will swell
till then

Galaxy

my earliest memory of it
a rhyme
innocent and naive
who knew the world that you orbit was to be
one of that that was obscene
repugnant and unfair
although how can your beauty compare
I stare at you with hope
that you would speak back
your light alludes
your luminosity lingers

It's just the circle of life

The circle of my life begins,
Round
Crack
At the sound of a quack
I open my brittle eyes with mother by side
To see the world, why it isn't so bad
Yellow
Dark
Changed
I grow and mother is gone
And it begins again
Round
Crack
I'm by their side

Thinking Game

My mind
a part of my body that holds so much
too much
without break and without a pause
I didn't sign up for it
if so, tell me which clause
says that I need to be switched on all the time
a constant wind
aches and pains
overthinking
what a tedious game

Game Day

Wish a rush of emotion
that momentous occasion where
with all the commotion
I burst into a rage
however pure
crowded by blood
I cheer on with relief
crying
ecstatic
joyous thrill
we won

Like a brick to my face

I always ponder about life
did I make mistakes
should I have this or that
oh the stakes
of being able to live the life you dreamed of
big house
luxuries
oh the dreams
but am I being vain
how can something as sinister as these dreams
cause me so much pain
I only wanted what was best
forgetting the rest
of the world who sit with crumbs
but happy
content
I wish I was as strong

Night Owl

When twilight hits
I know you're near
As if I've been holding my
breath all day
waiting
As the silence comes closer
it is my time
my heart settles
pound...pound...pound
I hear the beat finally...it's calm
no longer punching at my chest
rapid no more
crickets chirp
the nocturnal come alive
and it is in this time
im free
until the dawn blinds me back into reality
but for now
I'm free

Changes

Change is good they say
And although it may be
it's hard
I put up my guard
to the world around me
changing
please stop for a minute
to let me process
Changes
time stops
halt
I need a second to breathe
to think
to decide
Changes

Ask Me Maybe?

Ask me
What do I want?
Ask me
How do I feel?
Ask me
These societal pressures and constant
melodrama
Ask me
Did I ever want this?
The constant fear of not being wanted
Tell me
Do you understand?
how the world around me continues
to move on
whilst I stay in my cave
unconventional
burden
I'm sorry
but
please
for once
Ask me

Loners Midnight Mind

Two arms facing up
and I begin to ponder
wonder
what it may feel like to be
hugged
with true intention
kissed
with true passion
loved
with the purest heart
I do though?
Mom
Dad
but can I have more than that
am I worthy
Atleast I think so
but it's time to believe so

Sparkles

Diving into the whirlpool of light
I sigh
divinity
purest of heart
I smile
I reach out
bright
the constellations gaze below
linger and smile
I wish
a bow of heads at their ease
some day just
not yet

Slow Down

One moment here
Another there
Laughter
Pain
Happiness
Sadness
A perfect balance
Is hard to find
The world does not stop
for you
Ever
I say slow down
It speeds up
Please

Tired

I'm tired
of grief
I'm tired of pain
I'm tired of a world in which I receive
no gain
no movement
or improvement
Just meaningless anxiety

Electricity

Spark
Ignite
Control
What a power to behold
Without you a world so glum
However
Without you a world so strong

Cha Cha Cha

Teaching me the ways
of the Cha Cha Cha
One step you're here
another
you're there
the change in rhythm
we stride along
we adapt

What a Difference

And within seconds
what felt like a year
pain passes
and that feeling
is nothing like before
peace

A New Beginning

Curled
Light and cries
Hearing her voice
his voice
The first day
the first goodbye
Chapter 1
Grown and weary
Searching for companions
Chapter 2
Love
Chapter 3
A New Beginning
Full Stop

Never Settle

As thought the timer
suddenly halts
No...wait...I had more time
honest
I just checked
I was wrong
Did I make a mistake
Oh no
Do I ...but if I dont
what if?

And Here We Go

And here's to the nerves
the grievances
the trauma
Here we go
into the world
hurdle after hurdle
it's finally happening
the light in the tunnel
Here we go

And I Wonder

I wonder
Would life have been different?
I wonder
Would like be as tense?
I wonder
Would like be as selfishly straining
I wonder
What would it be like if we all just
gave
a
shit

Old Days

I miss the old days
where I would walk
miles
just to see my crush
reject my everlasting presence
I miss the days
I did my hair
to impress someone
who really wasn't impressed
rather was at pity
I miss the days
I message my friends to tell them
I spoke
to the one
I did
I miss the days where competition wasn't so
fierce
But all comes to an end
a stop
if it kept going would I have just
been treated
the same
no progress
I miss the old days
but I don't